CHEMICAL
DEPENDENCY

CHEMICAL DEPENDENCY

by ROBERT S. McGEE

Rapha Publishing
Houston, TX

Chemical Dependency
by Robert S. McGee
© 1991 by Rapha, Inc.

Scripture quotations are from the NEW AMERICAN STANDARD BIBLE, © The Lockman Foundation, 1960, 1962, 1963, 1968,. 1971, 1972, 1973, 1975, 1977.

Portions of *Rapha's Twelve-Step Program for Overcoming Chemical Dependency* reprinted and adapted by permission. Robert S. McGee with Pat Springle and Susan Joiner. (2d ed. © 1990 Rapha, Inc.)

Second Printing, 1992
ISBN: 0-945276-27-3
Printed in the United States of America

CONTENTS

INTRODUCTION

Addiction wears many faces; it has no respect for a person's age, race, sex, social standing, profession or religious belief. Some seem to be genetically predisposed to chemical addiction, and are "hooked" with the first drink, puff or pill. Others may abuse chemical substances for a number of years before crossing the line to dependency.

No one, however, plans on becoming chemically dependent. Addiction is usually the last thing on a person's mind when he takes his first drink or experiences his first high. Instead, he is most often thinking about being accepted by his peers, and about the glamour and excitement he perceives drinking or drugging will bring him.

If he gets hooked, the exuberance of his early association with alcohol or drugs will fade as the years pass. His drug of choice will become a reward for hard work, a remedy for anger, a means of controlling other people, a boost for his energy level, an escape from pain, a substitute for companionship, a self-prescribed aid to depression. His habit will become a need, and as it progresses, his life will begin to crumble. His drug of choice will no longer bring him a sense of freedom, but bondage, isolation, anxiety, fear and shame. He may experience broken relationships, the loss of a job, financial failure, declining health and a deteriorating self-esteem. Sadly, he (of all people) may be the last to see his addiction. Without help, he will probably die.

Why do people become chemically dependent? No one is really sure. What is known is that in addition to a complex interaction of cultural, environmental, interpersonal, intrapersonal and biological factors, the body of an addict cannot process alcohol or drugs normally. The presence of any chemical substance alters the cells in his nervous system, resulting in a craving for the substance, and withdrawal symptoms when it is taken away. [1]

It is estimated that one in every ten persons becomes chemically dependent, and that these people cannot stop drinking or using by themselves. While it does happen, it is generally a myth that the addict will have enough insight to see his condition and seek treatment for it.[2] It is also a myth to assume that addiction favors those on skid row. In actuality, only five percent of those who are chemically dependent live on skid row.[3]

Understanding these facts may enable you to see that addiction is very commonplace in society, and can happen to folks just like us, regardless of our reputation, social standing or religious beliefs.

WHY DOES A
PERSON ABUSE
ALCOHOL AND/OR DRUGS?

Chemical dependency typically evolves from abusing alcohol and/or drugs to meet a person's needs for comfort and esteem. In many cases, getting drunk or high begins as a mood-altering experiment which progresses to a repetitious coping mechanism for "getting along" with life. This is because chemical substances produce feelings of euphoria, especially in the early stages of use. As the pleasure centers of the brain "learn" this effect, impulses to use or drink gradually exceed the logic for not using or drinking. Defense mechanisms such as denial and repression sabotage decisions to quit. Finally, the user or drinker is addicted when the substance alters his brain chemistry so that the drug becomes vital to the brain's normal functioning.

Dysfunctional Families

Dysfunctional families, or families whose relationships don't function in healthy, productive ways, create tremendous hurts and needs in people's lives. Family dysfunction may be characterized by chemical dependency, workaholism, divorce, eating or sexual disorders, an emotionally and/or physically absent parent, neglect, verbal abuse, emotional, physical or sexual abuse, a domineering and/or passive parent, gambling or excessive spending. The impact of disorders like these may vary widely on each person within the family. The result, however, is that the family unit to some degree lacks the love, worth, stability and discipline its members need.

This chart illustrates some of the differences between healthy, functional families and dysfunctional families.[4]

Needs	Environment	Results	Motivation
Love Security Worth	Functional Family: love, acceptance, forgiveness, protection, oprovision, honesty, freedom to feel, loving discipline	Spiritual, Emotional, Relational Health: love, anger, fear, laughter, intimacy, willingness to take risks	Healthy Motives: love, thankfulness, obedience out of gratitude
Protection Provision	Dysfunctional Family (alcoholism, drug abuse, eating disorders, etc.): condemnation, manipulation, neglect, abuse, unreality, denial	Codependency: lack of objectivity, warped sense of responsibility, controlled/ controlling, guilt, hurt and anger, loneliness	Compulsive Motives: avoid pain, fear of rejection, fear of failure, gain a sense of worth, accomplish goals to win approval

Dysfunctional families leave many basic needs unmet. This usually leads to deep emotional pain, and often results in dependent and/or codependent behavior.

3

How Do Pain and Fear Contribute to Substance Abuse?

Much of our emotional pain comes from strained relationships—especially in our families—and from a poor perception of how to experience real love and significance. When we are born, we have very little perception of right and wrong, of truth and deception. Therefore, we usually accept whatever we are taught as truth. Our culture and many of our families teach us to value ourselves by our performance and the opinions of others. A formula for this teaching is:

Self-Worth = Performance + Others' Opinions.[5]

This perspective causes emotional pain and the fear of rejection and failure. It distorts our lives and can lead to:

- Being driven to succeed.
- Using alcohol or drugs to deaden feelings of pain and emptiness, or to ease the stress

often associated with maintaining a continually high level of performance.
- Being easily manipulated by others, manipulating other people.
- Doing whatever it takes to please people.
- Avoiding activities where the risk of failure or rejection are too great.
- Taking grave risks in the hope of succeeding and winning approval.
- Feeling depressed, lonely, ashamed and hopeless.
- Feeling self-inflated, invincible and indispensable.
- Blaming others or punishing them with ridicule, sarcasm or abuse.
- Exhibiting fear, anxiety, outbursts of anger, denial, repressed emotions.

The following test will give you some indication of how much you're affected by the need to perform and please others as the basis of your self-worth.[6]

Fear of Rejection or Failure Test

Read each of the following statements. From the top of the test, choose the term which best describes your response. Put the number above that term in the blank beside each statement.

1	2	3	4	5	6	7
Always	Very Often	Often	Sometimes	Seldom	Very Seldom	Never

_____ 1. Because of fear, I often avoid participating in certain activities.

_____ 2. I don't understand people and what motivates them.

_____ 3. When I sense that I might experience failure in some important area, I become nervous and anxious.

_____ 4. I always try to determine what people think of me.

_____ 5. I worry.

_____ 6. I become depressed when someone criticizes me.

_____ 7. I have unexplained anxiety.

_____ 8. I find myself trying to impress others.

_____ 9. I am a perfectionist.

_____ 10. I am critical of others.

_____ 11. I am compelled to justify my mistakes.

_____ 12. I am basically shy and unsocial.

_____ 13. There are certain areas in which I feel I must succeed.

_____ 14. It bothers me when someone is unfriendly to me.

_____ 15. I become depressed when I fail.

_____ 16. I am uncomfortable around those who are different from me.

_____ 17. I become angry with people who interfere with my attempts to succeed, and as a result, make me appear incompetent.

_____ 18. When I sense that someone might reject me, I become nervous and anxious.

_____ 19. I am self-critical.

_____ 20. I avoid certain people.

_____ Total (Add up the numbers you have placed in the blanks.)

Interpretation of Score

If your score is...

114-140

Your self-esteem is strong and positive, and you are not significantly affected by the fear of failure or rejection. (Or, you may lack objectivity about your thoughts, feelings and actions. Denial is common among people from addictive or abusive homes. They simply do not see themselves or others open-mindedly. If you scored in either of the two top categories (114-140 or 93-112), you might want your spouse or a close friend to take this test with you in mind for a more accurate reading.)

93-112

You are rarely affected by the fear of failure or rejection (or you lack objectivity to a significant degree).

73-92

When you experience emotional problems, they may relate to a sense of rejection or failure. Upon reflection, you will probably relate many of your previous decisions to these fears. Many of your future decisions will also be affected by the fears of failure and rejection unless you take direct action to overcome them.

53-72

Fears of rejection or failure form a general backdrop to your life. There are probably few days that you are not in some way affected by these fears.

0-52

Experiences of rejection or failure dominate your memory and have probably resulted in a great deal of depression. These problems will persist until some definitive action is taken. In other words, this condition will not simply disappear; time alone cannot heal your pain. You need to experience deep healing in your self-concept and in your relationships with others.

If your score falls in either of the last two categories, you are dealing with a lot of emotional pain. You may be susceptible to using alcohol and/or drugs as an escape and/or to fixing others' problems to win their approval.

STAGES OF ADDICTION

The downward spiral of addiction usually follows a predictable cycle which includes experimenting and learning, seeking, obsessing and consuming. Let's look at some characteristics of each of these stages:

■ *Stage One: Experimenting and Learning*
   In this stage, the user…
   • Is encouraged to try alcohol or drugs by peers, a counselor, dental or medical practitioner.
   • Personally desires acceptance and/or escape from pain—emotional and/or physical.

- Typically uses "light stuff" (alcohol, marijuana).
- Experiences euphoric effects of alcohol and/or drugs, usually with few consequences for using or drinking.
- Learns to trust the substance and its effects, and learns that those effects are controlled by amount of intake.

■ *Stage Two: Seeking*

Having learned that alcohol/drugs will produce "good" feelings, the user...

- Uses alcohol/drugs "socially."
- Establishes limits for drinking/using ("Two drinks are my limit." "I take my medication only as directed.").
- May use alcohol/drugs to excess occasionally and experience hangovers, blackouts or other physical manifestations of overdoing.
- Can usually continue to control the amount of alcohol/drugs he uses.

- May experience disruption in work or school as a result of drinking/using.
- Generally feels no emotional pain for choice to drink or use.

■ *Stage Three: Obsessing*

Alcohol/drugs become important, and in this stage, the user...

- Becomes preoccupied with getting "high."
- Develops compulsive approach to using/ drinking.
- Begins to experience periodic loss of control over alcohol/drug use.
- Breaks self-imposed rules about substance use established in stage 2, and increases drinking/using times and quantities.
- Loses sense of self-worth; begins to feel guilt and shame for behavior when high.
- Projects self-hatred onto others as health, stability, relationships and fellowship with God are adversely affected by using/ drinking.

- Begins to rationalize, justify and minimize negative feelings about himself.

■ *Stage Four: Consuming*

The substance "has" the user, and now he or she…

- Must use alcohol/drugs just to feel "normal."
- Believes other people and circumstances are the root of his problems.
- May entertain thoughts of additional escape possibilities such as suicide, leaving his family, moving out of town, etc.
- Experiences deteriorating physical health, as well as mental, spiritual and emotional health.
- Continually feels guilt, shame, remorse, anxiety, paranoia.
- Experiences withdrawal symptoms (nausea, vomiting, elevated blood pressure, sweating, depressed mood, anxiety, irritability, headaches, hallucinations, insomnia).

SYMPTOMS OF CHEMICAL DEPENDENCY

By definition, chemical dependency is the compulsion (forceful urge) to drink and/or use a chemical substance to achieve a desired effect, despite the experience of negative consequences for doing so. Codependency is the condition occurring when a person's God-given needs for love and security have been blocked in a relationship with a dysfunctional (dependent) person, resulting in a lack of objectivity, a warped sense of responsibility, being controlled and controlling others, hurt and anger, guilt and loneliness.[7]

Codependents often perpetuate addictive behavior by rescuing the dependent person from the consequences of his or her addiction. In a number of instances, individuals exhibit both chemically dependent and codependent behavior. Typically, persons who exhibit three of the following symptoms for a month's duration, or repeatedly over a longer period of time, are classified as chemically dependent.[8] These symptoms are:

1. Using a substance in larger amounts or over a longer period of time than originally intended.

2. Demonstrating an inability to reduce or control substance use, despite the desire to stop or cut back.

3. Spending large amounts of time in activities revolving around substance use, i.e., in obtaining, using and recuperating from the effects of the substance.

4. Being intoxified or suffering from withdrawal when expected to fulfill important obligations (work, school, home), or in situations when substance use is hazardous to himself and/or others (driving, piloting, operating machinery).

5. Giving up or avoiding important social, occupational or recreational activities to drink or use.

6. Continuing to drink or use after recognizing that substance use is contributing to physical, psychological, relational, financial, occupational or legal problems.

7. Taking increasingly larger amounts of a substance to achieve the same desired effect.

8. Experiencing withdrawal symptoms upon cessation or reduced intake of the substance.

9. Resuming or increasing substance use to relieve or avoid withdrawal symptoms.

Other primary symptoms that cause suspicion often associated with long-term substance abuse are:

- Wide mood swings: elated or depressed, omnipotent or sorry for oneself.
- New friends, peer group.
- Increased secrecy.
- Confusion, lethargy, bloodshot eyes, empty stares.
- Increased irresponsibility at home, work or school.
- Stealing, selling household items, gambling, shoplifting.
- Lying.
- Becoming defensive, demanding; argumentive over trivial things.
- Changing personal habits, clothing, weight, sleeping and eating habits.
- Inability to harmonize with friends, family, co-workers, authority figures.

The distinguishing mark of addiction is powerlessness. Initially, this may be difficult to grasp because the effect triggered by chemical substances is usually—with prolonged use—one of control. A person *thinks* he is in control when he is drinking or using. He is apt to feel out of control only when his drug of choice has been taken away and his comfort level begins to plummet. In reality, the sense of control he gains from drinking or using is a misconception.

There are usually two types of active addicts: those who know they are powerless over their dependency but cannot stop drinking or using, and those who cannot yet see their powerlessness over chemical substances.

One reason for this inability to recognize signs of powerlessness is the nature of drugs themselves. Chemical substances act on the central nervous system to produce feelings of euphoria, a lack of inhibitions and a sense of well-being. Some of these substances are accurately labeled pain killers. They not only deaden physical pain, but cross the emotional boundaries and deaden emotional pain as well. More often than not, the person suffering from chemical dependency is also suffering from such pain. Part of this is a result of the fact that his life, because of addiction, has become unmanageable. In an effort to block pain, the addict has built elaborately structured defense mechanisms which also prevent his seeing the truth about his addiction. This denial, combined with the numbing effects of chemical substances, makes it very difficult to perceive reality as it is.

Are You Chemically Dependent?*

Take the following test to help you determine if you are prone to alcohol or drug dependency. (You may want to repeat this test with a family member or friend in mind to help you determine if he or she has a significant problem with chemical

---

*Adapted from the Johns Hopkins Questionnaire.

dependency. You may also want someone else to take this test with you in mind.)

1. Do you lose time from work or school due to drinking or using drugs?
2. Is drinking or using making your home life unhappy?
3. Do you drink or use because you feel shy and insecure around people?
4. Is drinking or using affecting your reputation?
5. Have you ever felt remorse after drinking or using?
6. Have you gotten into financial difficulties as a result of drinking or using?
7. Do you turn to lower companions or an inferior environment when drinking or using?
8. Does drinking or using ever cause you to be careless about your family's welfare?
9. Has your ambition decreased since you've been drinking or using?
10. Do you crave a drink or feeling high at a definite time daily?

11. Do you want to drink or get high the next morning?

12. Does drinking or using cause you to have difficulty sleeping?

13. Has your efficiency decreased since you started drinking or using?

14. Is drinking or using jeopardizing your job?

15. Do you drink or use to escape from worries, troubles or feelings of rejection?

16. Do you drink or use alone?

17. Have you ever had a complete loss of memory as a result of drinking or using?

18. Has your physician ever treated you for drinking or using?

19. Do you drink or use to build up your self-confidence?

20. Have you ever been to a hospital or institution on account of drinking or using?

Answering yes to any one of these questions is a definite warning that you may be chemically dependent.

If you say yes to any two, you probably are chemically dependent.

If you answer yes to three or more, you definitely are chemically dependent.

EXPERIENCING RECOVERY

How Does a Person Experience Recovery?

How does one who is chemically dependent or codependent begin the process of effective, lasting change? The answer lies within the following six components:

Admit
New start
Support groups
Willingness
Education
Relapse prevention

Let's examine each of these elements of recovery:

Admit

By the time he becomes involved in treatment, the chemically dependent person usually knows he is hurting, and he may want help. But usually, he isn't able or willing to recognize his dependency as the culprit for his unhappy situation. Instead, he blames his boss or his parents, his spouse or his children, his circumstances or God. When he arrives at treatment, it is often with the idea that if he can get these people and/or circumstances straightened out, life will again be comfortable and he can continue drinking or using happily ever after.

Admitting powerlessness over the compulsion to get drunk or high is the first crucial step of recovery. Why? Because a person is not apt to invest himself fully in something he doesn't believe in, and staying clean and sober requires the kind of energy that must be backed by conviction.

Usually, however, no amount of logic or willpower can defeat chemical addiction until the dependent person is placed in a supportive care environment. This may include detoxification, inpatient or outpatient treatment, or daily attendance at support group meetings with a new routine which revolves around abstinence from substance use—all depending on the severity of his addiction.

If you are having trouble seeing and understanding the harmful effects of your addiction, or are working with someone who is, be patient. It takes time to develop objectivity and an open-minded attitude about something which has been perceived as necessary for someone's well-being for some time.

New Start

As we attempt to break free from a life-threatening habit, we have the opportunity for a new start in life. Developing some new, constructive habits in place of those that have proven to be self-defeating enhances our self-esteem. Habits that could contribute to our new start might be changing the route we take to work, to school, or home; varying our routine when we get up, come home, or get ready for bed; making new friends, perhaps with people who will contribute toward our recovery rather than our dependency.

We may need to seek out a more accurate concept of God, and place ourselves in situations where we can experience His love, forgiveness and strength. A better understanding of His character and motives for us usually helps us to gain a new attitude about accepting others and sharing ourselves with them. (Pages 39 to 48 explain how we can begin a relationship with Christ and/or experience a new start with Him.)

Support Groups

Personal reflection and application are most effective in an environment of affirmation and encouragement. This may include individual therapy, but you also need the support of others who have gone through (or are going through) this program of healing. This is especially important! It is extremely difficult—if not impossible—to overcome the painful causes and effects of addiction alone. Often, those closest to us (though they may mean well) have learned that our repeated promises to stop drinking or using mean nothing. They now may be understandably dubious that this time, we mean business. It will also take time for them to adjust to your new behavior. Those who have been where you are now understand. Let them help you!

Willingness

If your recovery is dependent on anything, it may be the degree of your willingness to get and stay clean or sober. To be willing is to be ready to act voluntarily. It is an attitude in action which says, *I'll do anything*, and then does just that.

In recovery, *anything* might be working through a 12-step program; attending a support group meeting on a daily basis for the first 90 days of recovery or admitting yourself to a structured inpatient or outpatient treatment program. *Anything* may mean gradually allowing other people to become involved in your life; being completely honest with yourself and others; considering a personal relationship with God; learning how to tolerate those people you might normally criticize.

Of course, you may have no desire to stop drinking or using because you have yet to see the need to do so. Give yourself some time. More importantly, give yourself an opportunity to cultivate the kind of willingness that will do *anything* to get better by investing yourself in a program of recovery.

Education

In many ways, recovery is simply a learning process about life and how to live it. To choose "real life" is to choose the experiences of joy and sorrow, love and grief, need and want, contentment and peace, victory and defeat.

If we're new to recovery, chances are that we know little about living "real life." Learning how to respond to life in a healthy way requires some education about our addiction to chemical substances: why we started drinking or using and how our addiction has affected us and others. Perhaps of the most immediate value is learning what triggers your compulsion to drink or use now. When do you especially want to get drunk or high, and why? Educating yourself with the answers to these questions will prolong your life!

As you grow in recovery, you will have opportunities to discover your emotions. It may now be difficult for you to differentiate between anger and grief, or love and affection. In time, however, you will gain a better understanding of your feelings and a greater appreciation for them.

With recovery comes an almost immediate awareness of needing people as never before. Interaction contributes to the satisfaction we sought unsuccessfully through drinking or using. In time, we will be able to embrace what we need to learn about building and enjoying healthy relationships.

Gradually, we also will learn that we choose our behaviors, and that every choice we make produces either a positive or a negative result.

As we grow, we will learn how to assume responsibility for our behavior, rather than allowing ourselves to be controlled by something or someone else.

Living in reality, we also will have an opportunity to learn more about God and to compare our new knowledge with our old conceptions about Him.

Of course, none of this can be learned in a day, or a week, or even a year. Perhaps one of the most valuable things we can begin teaching ourselves right now is to be patient while we're learning. Again, all of recovery is a learning process . . . it will take a lifetime to educate ourselves about productive ways of living and how to put that knowledge into practice.

Relapse Prevention

Studies show that 80 percent of those who enter recovery relapse within the first ninety days.

Relapse is returning to alcohol or drugs after a period of abstinence. Relapse is a possibility for anyone in recovery, regardless of how long he or she has been clean or sober. The reason this is true is because even though one has stopped drinking or using, he or she has not stopped having an addictive personality. When that addictive personality begins to control the recovering person's life, he or she is said to be a "dry drunk," one who has sobriety, but no serenity. In fact, the recovering person may exhibit all of the behaviors associated with his or her using or drinking days—without the presence of chemical substances.

33

■ **Warning Signals**

Like recovery, relapse is a process comprised of behaviors, attitudes, feelings, and thoughts which culminate in drinking or using. One may fall into a relapse over a period of hours, days, weeks, or even months.

Warning signals to alert you to a possible relapse are:

- Feeling uneasy, afraid, and anxious, sometimes about staying clean or sober. This begins to increase as "serenity" decreases.
- Ignoring feelings of fear and anxiety, and refusing to talk about them with others.
- Having a low tolerance for frustration.
- Becoming defiant, so that rebelliousness begins to replace what has been love and acceptance. Anger becomes one's ruling emotion.

- The "ISM" (I-self-me) attitude grows. Self-centered behavior begins to rule one's attitudes and feelings.
- Increasing dishonesty, whereby small lies begin to surface as deceptive thinking again takes over.
- Increased isolation and withdrawal characterized by missing groups and withdrawing from friends, family, and support.
- Exhibiting a critical, judgmental attitude, a behavior which is often a process of projection as the group member feels shame and guilt for his or her own negative behaviors.
- Overconfidence manifested by statements such as, "I'll never drink (or use) again," or by simply believing that one is the "exception" to all rules about recovery. He doesn't need to come to meetings anymore. She can handle going back to the old friends and places.

- Underconfidence about oneself manifested by self-derogatory remarks, overwhelming feelings of failure, a tendency to set oneself up for failure.

■ **Special Stressors**

In addition to these warning signals, it is important to be alert to certain times which can make one more vulnerable to relapse. Some of these include:

- Completing the first week of sobriety
- Completing the first twenty-one days of sobriety, and any anniversaries for sobriety thereafter, specifically: ninety days, six months, nine months, one year
- Holidays
- Personal anniversaries, birthdays, or other special days
- Experiencing "high" moods of exuberance, perhaps after receiving a raise, getting a job, getting engaged or married, etc. (Many people fail to

36

realize that "high" moods are as
stressful as low moods.)
• Becoming overly hungry, angry, lonely,
or tired

Heeding these warning signs will help you
stay on the path of recovery. Remaining in
relationships and situations which offer
accountability will strengthen and protect you.
Ask for help if you need it—your recovery is
truly a matter of life or death.

TRUSTING IN CHRIST

As has been stated before, chemical dependency (like other addictions) typically evolves from a person's attempt to meet his needs for comfort and esteem. At the root of these needs are deep longings to be fully known, loved, and accepted. It is not surprising that those who struggle with addictions also struggle—sometimes unaware—with deeper issues of neglect, abandonment, loss and/or abuse usually experienced in childhood.

Among all of the religions of the world, only Christianity offers the promise of meeting our deepest longings of the soul, because only Christianity focuses on a *relationship* with God. All other religions focus on performance.

Augustine observed, "Thou hast made us for Thyself, O God, and the heart of man is restless until it finds its rest in Thee." God desires to have an intimate relationship with us, and He has given us a provision for continual access to Him through His Son, Jesus Christ (John 3:16-17; Heb. 2:17). John 1:12 says, *But as many as received Him, to them He gave the right to become children of God, even to those who believe in His name.*

Are you trusting in your own abilities to earn acceptance with God, or are you trusting in the death of Christ to pay for your sins, and the resurrection of Christ to give you new life? Take a moment to reflect on this question: *On a scale of 0-100 percent, how sure are you that you would spend eternity with God if you died today?* An answer of less than 100 percent may indicate that you are trusting, at least in part, in yourself. You may be thinking, *Isn't it arrogant to say that I am 100 percent sure?* Indeed, it would be arrogance if you were trusting in yourself— your abilities, your actions and good deeds— to earn your salvation. However, if you are no longer trusting in your own efforts, but in the all-sufficient payment of Christ, then 100 percent certainty is a response of humility and thankfulness, not arrogance.

Reflect on a second question: *If you were to die today and stand before God, and He were to ask you, "Why should I let you into heaven?" what would you tell Him?* Would you mention your abilities, church attendance, kindness to others, Christian service, abstinence from a particular sin, or some other good deed? Paul wrote to Titus:

> *But when the kindness of God our Savior and His love for mankind appeared,*
> *He saved us, not on the basis of deeds which we have done in*

*righteousness, but according to His
mercy. . . .*

Titus 3:4-5

And to the Ephesians he wrote:

*For by grace you have been
saved through faith; and that not
of yourselves,
    it is the gift of God; not as a
result of works, that no one should
boast.*

Eph. 2:8-9

We must give up our own efforts to
achieve righteousness, and instead believe that
Christ's death and resurrection alone are
sufficient to pay for our sin and separation
from God.

In Acts 16:31, Luke wrote, . . .*Believe in
the Lord Jesus, and you shall be saved . . . .*
Jesus said: *I am the way, and the truth, and
the life; no one comes to the Father, but
through Me* (John 14:6).

42

We receive Jesus by invitation. He does not force Himself on us, but says:

> *Behold, I stand at the door and knock; if anyone hears My voice and opens the door, I will come in to him, and will dine with him, and he with Me.*

Rev. 3:20

Take some time to reflect on the two questions we examined on pages 40-41. Reflect on God's love, which He has expressed to you by sending His only Son to die in your place. Read Luke 22:39-46. Consider the selfless sacrifice of Jesus to carry out this divine plan. Realize that if you were the only person to walk this earth, Jesus would have done this for *you*.

If you are not 100 percent sure that you would spend eternity with God if you died today, and if you are willing to trust in Christ and accept His payment for your sins, you may use this prayer to express your faith:

43

Lord Jesus, I need You. I want You to be my Savior and my Lord. I accept Your death on the cross as payment for my sins, and now entrust my life to Your care. Thank You for forgiving me and for giving me a new life. Thank You for the new life that is now mine through You. Please help me grow in my understanding of Your love and power so that my life will bring glory and honor to You. Amen.

_____   _____

(signature)   (date)

If you have placed your trust in Jesus Christ prior to reading this, consider reaffirming your faith and commitment to serve Him. You may do so by using this prayer:

Lord, Jesus, I need You, and thank You that I am Yours. I confess that I have sinned against You, and ask You to "create in me a clean heart, and renew a steadfast spirit within me" (Ps 51:10). I renew my commitment to serve You. Thank You for loving me and for forgiving me. Please give me Your strength and wisdom to continue growing in You so that my life can bring glory and honor to You. Amen.

_____   _____

(signature)   (date)

It is important to understand that trusting in Christ does not guarantee an instantaneous deliverance from compulsive behavior or any other problem in life. However, it does mean that you are forgiven for your rebellion against

God; that you are restored to a relationship with Him that will last throughout eternity; and that you will receive His unconditional love and acceptance, as well as His strength and wisdom, as you continue to grow in recovery.

Baptism

Some people may ask, "How does baptism relate to one's conversion experience?" Water baptism is an outward demonstration of a believer's internal commitment to Christ. It enables the believer to identify himself with Christ in his culture. The act of baptism symbolizes his being dead, buried, and raised with Christ. In the early church and in some countries today, this identification is a dramatic statement of being severed from the world and being bonded to the body of Christ. In our society, it is still an important step of obedience as we identify ourselves publicly with Christ and His people. (For a sample of passages on Spirit or water baptism, see Acts 8:26-39; Rom. 6:1-4; and 1 Cor. 12:13.)

As a result of our trust in Christ, there are many facts and promises in God's Word that we can depend on. Facts are truths that are *already* true of us; *promises* are statements that we know will be fulfilled because of the trustworthiness of God. Here is a very short list of both:

Facts from God's Word

You are completely forgiven by God
    (Rom. 3:19-25; Col. 2:13-14).

You are righteous and pleasing to God
    (2 Cor. 5:21).

You are totally accepted by God
    (Col. 1:19-22).

You are deeply loved by God
    (1 John 4:9-10).

You are absolutely complete in Christ
    (2 Cor. 5:17; Col. 2:10).

The Holy Spirit dwells in you (Rom. 8:9-11).

You are God's child (Rom. 8:15-16).

You are a fellow heir with Christ (Rom. 8:17).

God works all things for good for those who love Him (Rom. 8:28).

Promises from God's Word

Christ will never leave us (Matt. 28:20; Heb. 13:5).

He will abundantly provide for our needs (Phil. 4:19).

We will be in heaven with Him (John 14:1-3).

We will reign with Him (2 Tim. 2:12).

He will strengthen us (Is. 40:29).

He will give us His peace (John 14:27).

He will accomplish His purposes (1 Thess. 5:24).

He will enable us to give generously (2 Cor. 9:6-11).

We will be persecuted (John 15:18-21).

HELPING SOMEONE WHO IS HURTING

How Do You Help Someone Who is Hurting?

It is often very difficult to help someone who is chemically dependent because he may not want help. Even if he does want help, his life may be in such shambles that it's hard to know where to start. Here are a few principles about helping someone who is hurting:[9]

Don't

1. Confront the person when he is drunk or high.
2. Yell, overreact, lecture or preach.

3. Let the person blame you for his or her behavior and its consequences. Don't blame yourself, either.

4. Accept excuses such as, "Everybody's doing it!"

5. Give orders or make empty threats. Follow through with what you say you will do.

Do

1. Act calmly. Communicate that you care. That's why you are getting involved.

2. Be objective. Don't exaggerate or deny the reality of the situation.

3. Plan ahead. Know what your options are. Know what you are going to do in a crisis situation so that you can tell him clearly and firmly about your plans when the situation occurs.

4. Get help. Contact someone who specializes in chemical dependency treatment and/or counseling.

Chemical dependency has debilitating, life-threatening consequences. A supportive care environment is essential to recovery. This may include outpatient treatment at a community health center, private therapy and/ or daily attendance at support group meetings. More severe cases may require hospitalization and detoxification. Some hospitals have units which specialize in treatment for chemical dependency. Ideally, medical care, proper nutrition, spiritual support, behavioral interventions, family education and support, individual and group therapy should be combined to help restore health and life satisfaction.

STAGES OF ACCEPTANCE

Despite the negative symptoms, consequences and complications of addiction, and the many benefits associated with recovery, many chemically dependent persons report profound feelings of loss at the onset of sobriety. Though these feelings eventually decline in frequency and intensity, they may last from several weeks to several years, depending on the severity of addiction.

One author has identified five stages experienced by those who are terminally ill.[10] Our observations have confirmed that those withdrawing from substance addiction usually

pass through similar phases at various
intervals during the recovery process:

- ***Denial***: Most chemically dependent
  persons are unable or unwilling to
  acknowledge their addiction—to
  themselves or others—despite obvious
  signs that they and their loved ones are
  suffering as a result of it.

  David was a dentist with a 15-year
  addiction to Demerol and codeine. When
  he lost his house, he blamed his wife.
  When his wife left him, he blamed his
  practice. When he lost his license, he
  blamed God, "who's had it out for me
  since the beginning." David was
  confronted several times about his drug
  problem. "Problem? What problem? I've
  just had a rough go of things," he said.
  Sadly, David remained unconvinced of
  his dependency. He eventually acquired
  AIDS as a result of using contaminated
  needles.

54

- **Bargaining**: Bargaining usually marks the beginning of the dependent person's recognition of his addiction, and is an attempt to postpone quitting. Bargaining can occur with oneself: "I need to kick this, but I'm just too restless right now. What's one more Valium? I'll quit later." Or, it can be a response to others: "Of course I'm still serious about quitting, and I will—right after this project at work blows over." Or, it can be a plea to God: "God, help me stop—tomorrow."

- **Anger**: When the chemically dependent person can no longer escape the facts pointing to his addiction, and/or when he finally enters treatment, anger is a normal response. Frequent objects of anger are God, family members or close friends, all of whom—according to the dependent person—contributed to his addiction or entry to treatment. His anger may also be directed toward others who are drinking or using (jealousy); the circumstances of needing to enter recovery; and anger with himself for perpetuating this perceived tragedy and for feeling helpless to overcome it alone.

- *Grief*: The majority of chemically dependent persons have become experts at avoiding painful emotions. The experience of deep distress, or grief, during recovery is often an unwelcome surprise.

    Many of us associate grief with the loss of a loved one, but feelings of grief are a normal response to the loss of anything we might consider important to our well-being.

    Substance abuse often provides an immediate payoff: It may calm a person's nerves; block feelings of pain, failure or disappointment; or give a person a sense of euphoria, courage, power or control. In addition, because the cycle of addiction turns a person increasingly inward, chemical substances often become a primary means of support. When this "support" is taken away, it's like losing a good friend. Grieving over such a loss is a normal, healthy aspect of recovery (even though it doesn't feel good), and is done properly when a person gives himself the freedom to feel loss whenever he is reminded of it.

- *Acceptance*: Over time, those who continue in recovery are able to accept their addiction and their need for treatment. Most are gradually able to accept a life apart from alcohol and/or drugs with serenity, and eventually, joy.

■ These stages often overlap in actual experience. Which one(s) are you in now? Describe your present feelings:

Recovery is a *process*. It is not like taking a pill or having a drink and then suddenly feeling better. Recovery is actually far more satisfying than that, and leads to a contentment and peace within that is *lasting*.

Along the way, you may discover that your addiction is a combination of different problems, but you also will have the satisfaction of seeing many of the problems that developed as a result of chemical abuse subside. Again, this will take time. Be patient with yourself. Be patient with those around you who may not be used to your new patterns of behavior. But above all, continue with the process. It really *is* worth it!

Editor's note:

At Rapha, we believe that small groups can provide a nurturing and powerful environment to help people deal with real-life problems such as depression, grief, fear, eating disorders, chemical dependency, codependency and all kinds of other relational and emotional difficulties. The warmth, honesty and understanding in those groups helps us understand why we feel and act the way we do. And with the encouragement of others, we can take definitive steps toward healing and health for ourselves and our relationships.

Not all groups, however, provide this kind of "greenhouse" for growth. Some only perpetuate the guilt and loneliness by giving quick and superficial solutions to the deep and often complex problems in our lives.

We urge you to find a group of people in your church, or in a church near you, where the members provide acceptance, love, honesty and encouragement. Rapha has many different books, workbooks, leader's guides and types of training so that people in these groups can be nurtured in the love and grace of God and focused on sound biblical principles to help them experience healing and growth.

To obtain a free list of the materials we have available, please write to us at:

Rapha, Inc.
8876 Gulf Freeway, Suite 340
Houston, TX 77017

NOTES

1. Hart, Larry, "Confronting Chemical Dependency in Your Church," *Mission Journal*, Feb., 1987, p. 4.

2. Johnson, Vernon E., *I'll Quit Tomorrow* (San Francisco, CA: Harper & Row, 1980), p. 1.

3. Spickard, Anderson, M.D., and Barbara R. Thompson, *Dying for a Drink: What You Should Know About Alcoholism* (Waco, TX: Word Books, 1985), p. 17.

4. Springle, Pat, *Codependency* (Houston and Dallas, TX: Rapha Publishing/Word, Inc., 2d ed., 1990) p. 21. Used by permission.

5. McGee, Robert S., *The Search for Significance* (Houston and Dallas, TX: Rapha Publishing/Word, Inc., 2d ed., 1990), p. 27.

6. Ibid. Adapted from pp. 46-47, 66-67.

7. Springle, *Codependency*, p. 23.

8. *The American Psychiatric Association, Diagnostic and Statistical Manual of Mental Disorders*, 3d ed., Rev. (Washington, D.C.: The American Psychiatric Association, 1987), adapted from pp. 166-67.

9. Adapted from the Crestview Center, Anderson, IN.

10. Kübler-Ross, Elisabeth, *On Death and Dying* (New York: MacMillan Publishing, 1969).

ABOUT THE AUTHOR...

Robert S. McGee is a professional counselor and lecturer who has helped thousands of people experience the love and acceptance of Jesus Christ. He is also the Founder and President of Rapha, a nationally recognized health care organization that provides in-house care with a Christ-centered perspective for adults and adolescents suffering with psychiatric and substance abuse problems. The truths presented in his book, *The Search for Significance*, form the foundational cornerstones that provide the balance of spiritual and clinical therapy in the Rapha Treatment Centers program.

He is also the author of *Discipline with Love* and co-author of several books, including *Rapha's 12-Step Program for Overcoming Chemical Dependency*, *Rapha's 12-Step Program for Overcoming Eating Disorders*, *Your Parents and You*, *Bitterness*, and *Getting Unstuck*.